BRITAIN IN OLD PHOTOGRAPHS

CANNOCK CHASE
PAST & PRESENT

HERITAGE INDEPENDENT

PHOTOGRAPHERS

SUTTON PUBLISHING LIMITED

Sutton Publishing Limited
Phoenix Mill · Thrupp · Stroud
Gloucestershire · GL5 2BU

First published 1996

Cover photographs: Cannock town centre,
looking north from Market Place.

British Library Cataloguing in Publication Data

A catalogue record for this book is available from the
British Library.

ISBN 0-7509-0865-3

Typeset in 10/12 Perpetua.
Typesetting and origination by
Sutton Publishing Limited.
Printed in Great Britain by
Ebenezer Baylis, Worcester.

CONTENTS

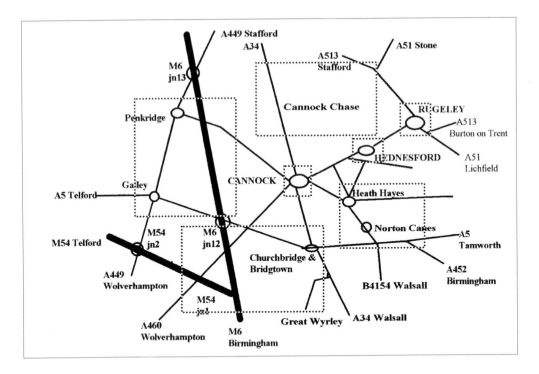

detailed sketch maps for these areas appear
at the beginning of the relevant section

A comprehensive street map covering Cannock, Hednesford and Rugeley in
detail is available from Cannock Council Offices or the Tourist Information
Centre at the Valley Heritage Centre together with a guide for the area.

THIS PUBLICATION HAS BEEN SUPPORTED BY

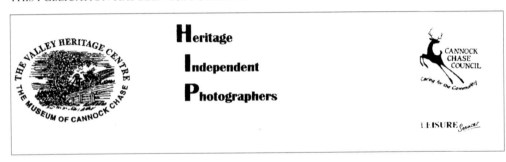

INTRODUCTION

This book grew out of a project that Heritage Independent Photographers undertook for the Valley Heritage Centre starting in the autumn of 1993 to produce an exhibition of photographs comparing images from the archive with the current scene.

The exhibition held in the winter of 1994 proved such a success, over 2,000 visitors in two months, that a second show was planned for early 1996. This exhibition was opened by international photographer Richard Saddler FRPS, and also proved to be a huge success. Many requests for a book were received so Heritage Independent Photographers and the Valley Heritage Centre approached Sutton Publishing.

While the concept for the project appeared straightforward, putting it into practice proved more difficult than the members of HIP anticipated. Starting with the prints in the VHC archive, which includes a set of originals taken and printed by A.D. Orton snr between 1900 and 1905, a copy negative was made of each. This enabled new working prints to be made thus protecting the originals.

The next stage was to find the locations so that the current scene could be recorded. This was when the problems started. Many of the locations were obvious but the information for some was, to say the least, scant. For instance the photograph in the Hednesford section of a man in the road was noted as just that, 'a man in the road'. When inquiries were made as to the road in question several sites were given, resulting in several locations being visited before the photograph on page 88 was made. Even when the location was not in doubt problems could arise if the viewpoint used by the previous photographer was no longer accessible. When this happened the nearest viewpoint was used, or the prevailing atmosphere was shown.

The way that photographers worked in the past proved interesting. At the turn of the century, when Mr Orton was taking his photographs, the equipment, or apparatus as cameras were referred to then, was cumbersome. Glass plates in wooden holders were used in cameras with wooden bodies standing up on wooden tripods. The weight of a small apparatus could be several pounds. Transporting this bulk must have been a problem. Motor vehicles were not common so one presumes that a pony and trap or even a push-bike was used. This led to photographers setting up their apparatus and then taking several shots from the same position, usually turning the camera through 90 or 180 degrees. Look closely at some of the Cannock town centre images to see examples of this.

Given the limitations of the equipment used the results achieved by the old photographers have to be admired. Lenses were simple, emulsions were slow and of limited colour sensitivity, which would have resulted in fairly long exposures even in good light. By the end of the Great War life would have been getting easier, as glass plates had been superseded by sheet film. Roll film was gaining in popularity with cameras becoming smaller and lighter; even so a pocket camera of the mid-'20s taking eight 3.5 in x 2.25 in exposures could measure 8 in x 3 in and be nearly 2 in thick and weigh about 2 lbs. Pockets must have been much larger in the past!

An unusual and interesting feature of many of these early photographs is the way the lenses used reproduced the view. The front of the Five Ways public house on page 32 is a classic example. In the old photograph the front of the building is square on to the camera and both sides of the building are visible; in the modern version the front is still square on but you cannot see as much of the sides. It is as if the angle between the sides has become narrower. Several attempts were made using a wide variety of lenses from semi-wide angle to telephoto and with different cameras from 35 mm to 5 in x 4 in monorail, the latter being near to the probable equipment used to take the original image. It proved impossible to reproduce this effect.

Another phenomenon which soon became apparent was the tremendous increase in the number and size of trees. We tend to think that there has been a decrease in the tree population but from the evidence of these photographs the reverse is happily the case. The greatest increase appears to have taken place in the urban areas. The tree types on the Chase have changed over the years with the even ranks of Forestry Commission pine plantations taking over from open heath and deciduous woods. This increase in trees caused some problems with viewpoints; in some cases the scene has been retaken as faithfully as possible if the main subject is still reasonably visible. If this was not the case a viewpoint which reflected any change has been used.

As one would expect, the changes that have occurred can be dramatic or very subtle. Cannock and Rugeley both appear to have had dramatic changes but if one looks above the modern corporate shop facias the old buildings remain. This process is still going on. Since the photographs for this book were taken in early 1996 the centre of Cannock has seen a new shopping mall and a new bank appear.

Each section begins with a sketch map and we hope that you will enjoy finding the locations and making your own mind up as to whether the changes have been for the better. The Ordnance Survey Explorer 6 map with a scale of 4 cm to 1 km (2½in to the mile) will prove to be a great help in finding your way around the area.

Should you have any detailed information regarding any of the sites shown in *Cannock Chase Past and Present* the staff at the Valley Heritage Centre would be interested in hearing from you. It would be preferable to put your comments in writing addressed to: The Curator, Valley Heritage Centre and Museum of Cannock Chase, Valley Road, Hednesford, Staffordshire, WS12 5QX. A stamped addressed envelope would be appreciated if a reply is required. Anyone interested in joining Heritage Independent Photographers should also apply in writing with a stamped addressed envelope care of the above address.

Finally, for those interested in technicalities the modern images were mainly taken on Fuji or Bronica 645 cameras; other equipment used ranged from 35 mm Leica to 6 x 6 Mamiyaflex. All the processing and printing was done by group members in their own darkrooms.

ACKNOWLEDGEMENTS

Heritage Independent Photographers have had the help and advice of many people in producing this book. They extend special thanks to the following:

Adrienne Whitehouse and all her staff at the Valley Heritage Centre for all the hours and help so willingly given, and for the access to the Centre's archive. To their wives and girlfriends who have put up with them regularly disappearing to take photographs when the light was right, and into the darkroom to print the photographs. To Mrs B. Fearns for the loan of the postcard on page 34.

The photographs from the Valley Heritage Centre collection taken between 1900 and 1910 by Mr A.D. Orton snr are page 18, lower photo on page 37, upper photos on pages 45, 47, 49, 50, 51, page 52 and 58, upper photos on pages 60, 61, 62, 63, 64, and 70.

The following photographs have been generously donated to the Valley Heritage Centre: upper photos on pages 11, 15, 16, page 18, upper photos on pages 20, 23, 26, 28, 32, 54, 55, 68, 71, 75, 84, 86, 87, page 92, upper photo on page 99, page 114, upper photos on pages 116, 125 and 126 by Mr John Godwin; page 72 by B. Tongue; upper photos on page 75 and 123 by R.H. Hodgson.

The remaining old photographs have been donated to the Valley Heritage Centre by many people and organizations too numerous to list, to whom we give thanks for their generosity.

Finally, thanks to all the people on the Chase who gave their knowledge and advice, and for their interest in the project.

Photographs by
Heritage Independent Photographers

Text edited by
Tony Middleton

The members of HIP. Left to right:
Mike Brownridge, Patrick Hickey, Tony Middleton, Andrew Biggs, Stan Hussey.

Heritage Independent Photographers is a group of photographers with a wide range of backgrounds who are based at the Valley Heritage Centre, Hednesford. The group aim is to provide photographers who are producing personal work a forum in a non-competitive environment. Regular meetings are held at the Valley Heritage Centre where members can show and discuss their current work. In addition to producing archive material and exhibitions for the centre upon mutually agreed themes individuals also produce their own exhibitions with the help and support of group members.

CANNOCK TOWN CENTRE

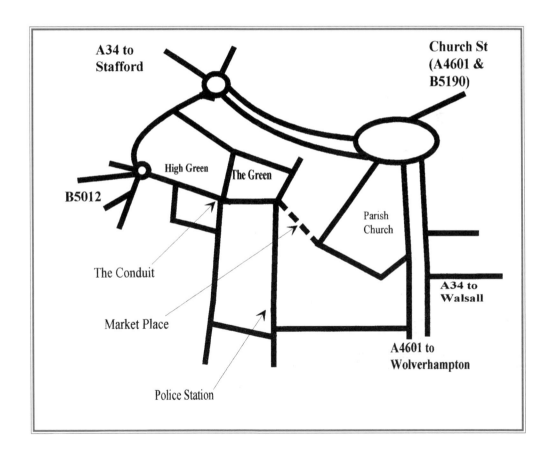

Dating back to Domesday, Cannock has always been the major settlement in the area. It came into prominence during the seventeenth and eighteenth centuries as a healthy place for the more well-off to live. The waters of Cannock were popular but never achieved the prominence of Cheltenham, Leamington or Buxton. This accounts for the number of large houses which were built in the area; several still survive but sadly many have been demolished.

The population probably did not exceed 1,000 until after the mid-nineteenth century when coal became the mainstay of the region's economy. Coal had been surface mined for many years but the advent of deep mining caused a population explosion and the town grew rapidly.

Communications had to improve as the reputation of Chase coal spread and the rail and canal networks steadily grew. Roads appear to have developed at a slower pace as there was not an economical means of transporting the heavy loads that could be handled by rail and narrow boat. Of course the reverse now applies: road transport dominates and the area is bisected by the M6, rail is a recently reintroduced and heavily subsidised commuter service, while canals are purely for pleasure.

Cannock underwent major changes in the 1960s and early '70s, the Crown Hotel, Market Hall and several other buildings being demolished to make way for a modern shopping area which is now (August 1996) being redeveloped.

The Green and High Green have seen fewer changes. The bowling green has been in constant use for over 180 years, and the eighteenth-century mansion house, which used to be the Council House, remains much as it appeared in the late nineteenth century. The Conduit or Tank House dates from 1736 and was the outlet for Cannock's first regular water supply.

Mill Street, Cannock, looking north, *c.* 1910.

Looking north across Market Place. St Luke's Church is to the right.

From approximately the same viewpoint used on page 11 turn to your left, and you will see the Yorkshire Bank on the site formerly occupied by D.W. Clarke & Son.

On the opposite corner and a little way down Walsall Road is the last remaining cinema in Cannock. The upper photograph shows it in its heyday, 1937, when a visit to the pictures was the highlight of the week.

Market Place has always been the hub of Cannock. Built in the reign of Queen Anne (1702–14), the Crown Hotel was demolished in 1962. The Market Hall on the left suffered a similar fate and was replaced with modern shops.

The opposite side of Market Place has not undergone such a dramatic change in appearance. The shop fronts and signs have changed but the buildings remain substantially unaltered.

Market Place looking towards High Green. Apart from the addition of the fountain in the late '80s the scene is little different from the earlier photograph, which was probably taken in the '50s.

Leading off Market Place is Wolverhampton Road. This used to be one of the main roads leaving Cannock. Imagine it coping with the traffic which now uses Avon Way.

The Old Law Courts, on the site now occupied by the police station.

The modern police station.

The upper photograph shows Dr Butter's house being demolished. Originally it was Cannock's police station. The current building can be seen under construction on the right.

Wolverhampton Road looking towards Market Place.

Looking across the bowling green, reputed to be one of the best in England, to High Green.

The view looking south to Market Place from High Green.

The Conduit, a unique hexagonal brick building with a pyramid roof, housed the outlet of the pipe which supplied the town with water from a spring at Rummer Hill. On the opposite corner is one of the oldest buildings in Cannock, which used to be Linford's hardware shop.

The old post office, built in 1908 and replaced by the present office in Mill Street. Adjoining it is the New Hall, dating from 1890. Once a Sunday school, it was later a gymnasium and then a working men's institute, known as Skinners as most of its members were skint or penniless. Since the current photograph was taken it has changed once more, from a frozen food shop to a fabrics shop.

Mill Street has changed dramatically from the upper photograph, with its thatched cottage, to the modern dual carriageway, part of the town's ring road.

Cannock station was opened in 1858 and fell victim to the Beeching cuts in the '60s. The new station is part of a commuter link, opened in 1989, to Birmingham, reflecting the dormitory role of the town.

Belgrave House on the New Penkridge Road (B5012) was once a desirable residence. Now it has been denuded of its trees and is used as offices.

HEATH HAYES, BURNTWOOD & NORTON CANES

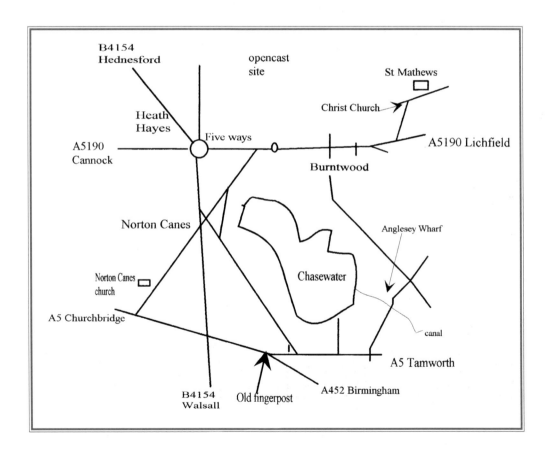

These three villages lying to the west of Cannock represent different types and rates of development. Heath Hayes and Norton Canes grew as the mining developed but in different ways; Burntwood was mainly a farming community.

Heath Hayes developed in a wedge shape, with the point at Five Ways and development taking place to the west between the main Cannock Road (A5190) and Wimblebury Road. The main shopping area grew along the Hednesford Road which bisects this wedge. There were no main mines in the village but several around its perimeter.

Norton used to be concentrated around the church near Watling Street (A5) as shown in the first Ordnance Survey map. But as the Jerome family, of *Three Men in a Boat* fame, developed the deep mine in the centre of the present village, the population moved to the north side of Watling Street. This development joined the three distinct settlements, Norton, Norton East and Norton Leys, now jointly known as Norton Canes – a corruption of Norton-under-Cannock.

Burntwood was on the eastern edge of the South Staffordshire coalfield and retained much of its rural atmosphere until commuter housing started after the Second World War. The present Burntwood contains several previously autonomous villages and has moved south of its original centre.

Stables at Anglesey Wharf.

The Primitive Methodist church, Hednesford Road, Heath Hayes. Methodism was very strong in the mining areas at the turn of the century. The church has lost its bell tower and the chimney at the rear; otherwise the building is nearly original.

Just as churches have withstood change so have many of the area's pubs. The Five Ways Inn looks the same as it did before the Great War and is still a place to go to have a drink and a chat. Darts and dominoes are still popular. Real pubs like this are still to be found on the Chase.

On the opposite corner stands the old cinema, now a carpet warehouse. The distinctive semi-circular roof has gone and it has been extended each side on the first floor, but it still has the unmistakeable air of a cinema.

Between the wars the postcard was the means of mass communication: today we would pick up the telephone to arrange a meeting. In 1937 Jack sent this card to Betty to say he would see her on Friday. The change in attitudes to mental health shows on this card. St Matthew's Hospital is bluntly called the 'Asylum'. The centre photograph is Christ Church, which has now lost its ivy cladding.

The left-hand pair of photographs on the postcard opposite show Cannock Road (A5190) looking east and the front of the main building of St Matthew's Hospital, which is now closed. There are plans to develop this site for high-class housing, but this frontage is listed and should survive.

The right-hand pair of photographs on the postcard on page 34 show the Cannock Road in the opposite direction to the previous shot, together with the entrance to St Matthew's.

An earlier composite postcard showing four views of Norton Canes. The modern views follow on pages 38 and 39.

An earlier shot of St James's church, which is now impossible to re-photograph from the same viewpoint as a house has been built on the site.

The Square, Norton Canes, has changed little over the years – unlike Chapel Street. The chapel has been replaced by a group surgery for local doctors.

Norton Pool, the smaller of the two parts of Chasewater, known locally as 'The Swag'. This view was marred by an electricity pylon standing on the grassed area in the foreground until it was demolished in 1992.

St James's as it appears today. The original church was built in 1832 and the present one in 1888 after a fire.

The oldest signpost in England was situated at the junction of Watling Street and the Chester road (A5 and A452). It is reputed to date from 1777. The original shown above is now housed in the Staffordshire County Museum at Shugborough Hall.

The modern facsimile of the original fingerpost.

Anglesey Wharf at the southern end of Chasewater on the Wyrley and Essington canal. The loading chutes for the coal from the Chasetown pits can still be seen. Up to the '50s narrow boats were pulled by heavy horses: today the only sign of this once hard way of life is some overgrown crumbling brickwork from the stables in the hedge behind the chutes.

GREAT WYRLEY, CHURCHBRIDGE, BRIDGTOWN & WEDGES MILLS

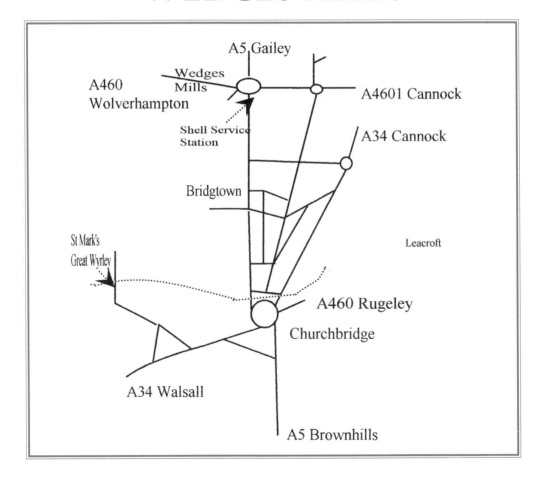

A5 Gailey

Wedges Mills

A460 Wolverhampton

A4601 Cannock

A34 Cannock

Shell Service Station

Bridgtown

St Mark's Great Wyrley

Leacroft

A460 Rugeley

Churchbridge

A34 Walsall

A5 Brownhills

Great Wyrley and Churchbridge are long established villages which mainly depended upon brick and tile production. In the 1880s Churchbridge gained in importance owing to its position at the crossroads of Watling Street (A5) and the main road from the Potteries to the north and Birmingham. The main employer for many years was the Edge Tool works founded by William Gilpin on the site now occupied by Britool.

Bridgtown grew as Cannock expanded with the rise of deep mining and the need for housing, an early example of suburban growth. The different areas have slowly expanded and joined together and the boundaries are no longer obvious. Small enterprising firms now abound in the maze of streets on the north side of the A5, while large international companies and retail parks are found on the south side of the road.

The complex of road islands at the junction of the A5 and A34.

St Mark's Church, Great Wyrley. The upper photograph, taken between 1900 and 1910, shows an overgrown and neglected churchyard. Today the churchyard is a pleasant open grassed area, with a garden of remembrance to the right of the main doorway.

North-east of Churchbridge is Leacroft. The area is now dominated by Sainsbury's, the Orbital Retail Park and a landfill site. Leacroft colliery was on the northern side of this area.

Extensive opencast mining took place between Churchbridge and Norton Canes in the '70s and '80s, the site being known as Kingswood. Leacroft Hall, the entrance to which is shown in the upper picture, was on the site now occupied by a motorbike scrambling course and a golf driving centre. The reclaimed land has largely been returned to farming, but is now featureless and lacking in established trees.

On the opposite side of the new dual carriageway is Mid Cannock Colliery. In 1945 this colliery was producing 212,000 tons of saleable coal. The modern plant processes the coal extracted by opencast mining at Bleak House to the north of the A5190 at Five Ways. This coal is transported to the processing site by lorries using a specially constructed road across the old Kingswood opencast workings.

There are two railway bridges built by the South Staffordshire Railway at Churchbridge, one across the A5 and another across the A34. For some reason, only known to himself, Mr Orton chose to record the latter sometime between 1900 and 1910. The bridge now bears the scars made by heavy lorries which have misjudged the height of the arch.

Maybe on the same day Mr Orton took this photograph of the road on the far side of the bridge. The major difference in today's image is that the road surface has improved. The slip road leading to Bridgtown, and the buildings beyond, have not changed very much.

Bridgtown church in East Street, *c.* 1905. This corrugated steel building has twice been replaced. The present Bethel Methodist church is the third on this site.

The United Methodist church at the corner of Park Street and Union Street: another church study by Mr Orton.

Today this building houses Midland Commercial Pressings Ltd. The belfry has been removed together with the foundation stones.

Longford Island at the junction of the A5 and A460. The motor-car has been the catalyst for many of the changes shown in this book and nowhere is its effect more marked than at Longford Island. The only similarity between the garages is that both are selling Shell fuel.

Workmen's dwellings, built in about 1795 at Wedges Mills. They were demolished during road widening in the early '50s.

Hilton Hall. There is evidence of settlements on this site predating Domesday. The present building was built in the early seventeenth century by Henry Vernon as a two storey L-shaped mansion. The upper storey shown in both these photographs was added in 1829 by Major-General Graham. This addition together with some other lesser alterations cost £18,000. The upper photo dates from the early twentieth century. In the mid-'50s the Vernons sold the hall to a Mr Pickard of Pelsall. In 1958 it became a guest house for the elderly run by the Sisters of St Joseph. The nuns put the hall on the market in 1981, and Tarmac plc purchased the property in 1985 as its group head office and undertook an extensive restoration programme. The building is not open to the public.

FOUR CROSSES, GAILEY & PENKRIDGE

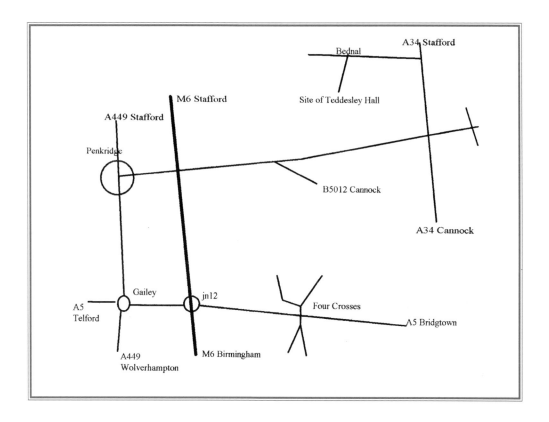

Four Crosses grew around the coaching inn on the Watlington Street, and remains a farming community. Gailey, like many villages along the A5, owes its existence to being at a crossroads. The main road from Stafford to Wolverhampton (A449) crosses the A5. But before this there was a Romano-British settlement, *Pennocrucium*, to the west of the junction.

Penkridge is now a pleasant commuter town with a quaint main shopping street. There is still a thriving traditional market twice a week, the origins of which go back to a charter granted by Henry III in 1244. Staffordshire was a centre for horse sales and Penkridge was the major market at the turn of the century. The river Penk meanders through the fields to the north of the village and there are some good walks along its banks and the neighbouring canal.

The oldest house in Penkridge, *c.* 1910.

The Four Crosses Inn has undergone some subtle changes between the upper picture from the '30s and the lower one taken in 1995. The left-hand brick-built part of the inn has not noticeably changed, but the timber work in the present building is far more elaborate than the original.

St Saviour's Church on the opposite side of the A5 to the Four Crosses Inn is not as different as it looks in these two photographs. The early photograph, probably dating from the '30s, shows some ornate brickwork over the door. This still exists under the new outer brick skin that was built in front of the existing walls in the late '50s. The top row of bricks on each side of the church is bevelled under the guttering which is attached to the original wall.

Pool House, Gailey, even though it stood beside Watling Street, would have been reasonably tranquil when the upper photograph was taken by Mr Orton at the beginning of the century. To have reproduced Orton's picture exactly would have entailed standing in the middle of the present A5 trunk road, not something to be recommended, even for historical accuracy!

The Victorian church at Gailey was built by G.T. Robinson in 1849 and extended in 1874 by James Fowler of Louth. Now de-consecrated, the building houses a pottery and craft centre.

St Michael and All Angels, Penkridge, was one of six collegiate churches in Staffordshire before the Reformation. The interior of this splendid local red sandstone church contains some interesting tombs and monuments to the Littleton family.

Teddesley Hall was built in the eighteenth century by William Baker for the Littletons. The main structure was demolished shortly after the Second World War leaving the two buildings on each side, which are now used for storage. A Snetzler organ which was in the house was moved to St Andrew-by-the-Wardrobe in the City of London.

CANNOCK CHASE

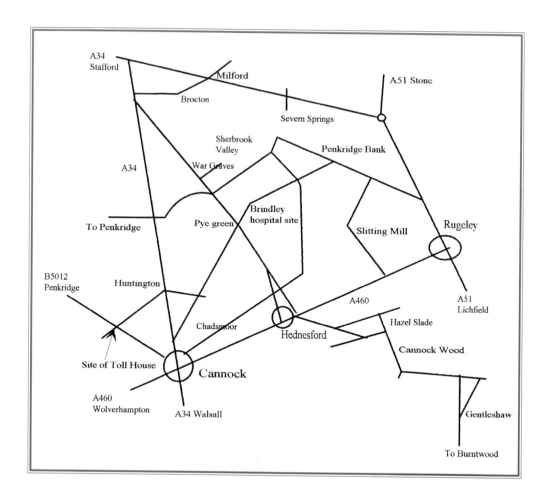

The present 20,000 acres of the Chase is a shadow of its original size but it is still a place of contrasts. Milford Common on the A513 is a popular, bustling spot at weekends. Impromptu games of cricket or football, ice-cream vans, fast food and a busy pub set the scene. Walk less than half a mile into the hills behind the Common and there is peace and tranquillity. This northern half of the Chase is rolling heather and bracken covered hills with broad leafy woods, which contrast with the southern half which is mainly Forestry Commission plantations. Sherebrook valley forms a natural boundary between the two.

Wildlife abounds on the Chase. Fallow deer, thought to have been introduced by the Bishops of Lichfield in the eleventh or twelfth century, are common, together with smaller numbers of red deer. They are reasonably easy to see in the early morning or evening, especially in the ancient Brocton Coppice or along Sherebrook valley. Unfortunately the roads across the Chase are fairly straight and many motorists travel too fast, not realising the danger the deer present. Hitting even a small deer at forty miles an hour can kill or seriously injure it and the damage to the vehicle will be substantial. One of the rarities to be heard, and seen if you are lucky, is the nightjar, which breeds in small numbers on parts of the Chase. You may also see foxes, badgers, rabbits, skylarks, kestrels and rare plants, such as the two types of insectivorous sundew.

The Chase was used for training in both world wars, and today has both the Commonwealth and German military cemeteries with the Katyn memorial to Polish officers massacred by the Russians. The Great War camp's remains can be explored using a leaflet issued by the Ranger Service, whose visitor centre is located on part of the Second World War RAF camp.

Wandon Lodge.

Shoal Hill is half a mile north-west of Cannock on the B5012 to Penkridge. Behind the modern armco barriers the posts and rails clearly shown in the upper photograph can still be found. They were known as the Monkey Rails. The locals used to meet here after church or chapel and many a marriage resulted. The name came from the local nickname for miners, 'struggling monkeys'. Another story to explain the name is that the union men would meet on the common out of the sight and hearing of the bosses.

Old Toll House, nr. Cannock.

At the crossroads on the northern edge of Shoal Hill stood the Old Toll House, which was demolished in the '50s.

Hatherton Hall was rebuilt in 1817 by the Walhouse family, who married into the Littleton family and became the Lords Hatherton. The family moved to Teddesley Hall (see section four) and Hatherton Hall is now in private hands. Views of the stucco exterior with its pinnacles and castellations can be had across the fields from the lane between Shoal Hill and Hatherton village.

Heath Farm, Huntington, *c.* 1905. It is recalled in the name of this new housing estate off the A34.

The Great War military hospital at Brindley Heath, started in 1916, had 1,000 beds in 12 wards. Each ward was 208 ft x 20 ft, spaced at 25 ft intervals along a corridor. After the war it was used by the Ministry of Pensions and was finally closed in 1924. The site was then used by miners and their families, who built a school, social club and other essentials. In the 1950s they were rehoused in the estate off Broadhurst Green and Bradbury Lane. This estate is still known as Brindley Village.

SEVEN SPRINGS, CANNOCK CHASE

This is one of those photographs which make you wonder if the postcard photographer got his notes mixed up. The above card is clearly labelled Seven Springs, but after several hours walking the area and showing this card to many walkers it was not possible to reproduce this scene. So the opportunity has been taken to show two typical views of the Chase on the opposite page. The upper one is the path leading from the car-park at Seven Springs to Haywood Warren. Sherebrook valley in the lower picture offers some of the best scenery on the Chase with reasonably easy walking. The Great War Brocton camp was situated on the top of the hills on the left and traces of the firing ranges can be found in the woods on the right.

Milford station, 1920s. During the Great War this was one of the main stations from which the troops marched up to Brocton camp. As with many small stations this one has not withstood progress and the electrified main line trains from the north-west to London now rush by without stopping.

The other main camp during the Great War was Rugeley camp, which was situated to the east of Brindley Hospital. Troops and materials arrived for this camp at Rugeley Trent Valley station. The goods were transported by lorry and the troops marched the 4 miles to the camp along Penkridge Bank, the road shown in these photographs.

The main road across the Chase is the Cannock to Rugeley A460. These shots show it just north of Hednesford. The gentleman with his push-bike would not pose for his photograph in the middle of the modern road. The HIP photographer had parked his car and stood in front of it to get the lower picture.

The racing stables at Hazel Slade, from which three Grand National winners emerged between 1907 and 1931. They are now being converted into dwellings.

Cannock Wood colliery, once one of the major pits in the area and now used as an industrial estate. However, some of the original buildings are still in use instead of just the more usual rows of identical units.

The Windmill public house at Gentleshaw is one of the oldest on the Chase. George Heggs, Jack Fisher, Jess Bradbury and Jim Southall are shown enjoying a well-earned drink. Today the Windmill still offers hospitality, good food and drink. No doubt the interior has changed but the four in the early photograph would probably still recognize the exterior.

Chadsmoor grew between the wars and the Central cinema was the main place of entertainment for most families. The frontage has gone but the main auditorium is now used as a tile showroom.

HEDNESFORD

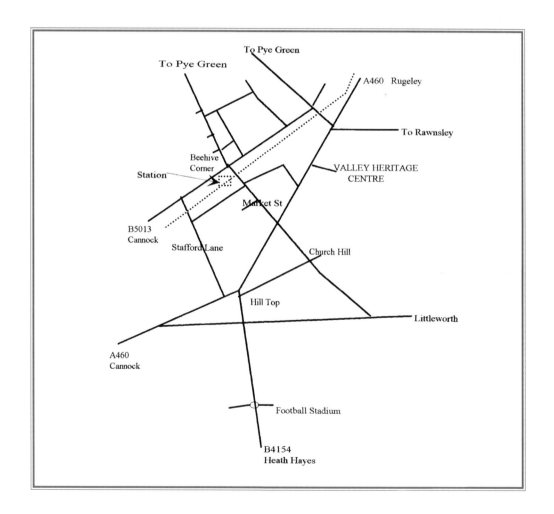

This is the largest section in the book. As the Valley Heritage Centre is in the town, the archive contains a large selection of material on Hednesford and the surrounding area. Hednesford is another example of a village which has moved its centre and in the process has become a town. Early Hednesford centred on the Cross Keys; this area between the inn and Hill Top is known as Old Hednesford. When mining started to develop the centre moved to between the main road from Cannock to Rugeley and the new railway station. From the mid-1880s Hednesford grew rapidly with deep mines on all sides of the town. Some of these mines are now enterprise centres, and new high-tech industries are being started.

This development to one side of a major road has given the town a distinctive atmosphere. There must be many who rush by on the A460 thinking that Hednesford has little to offer: how wrong they are. The shops still offer personal service and there is a friendly buzz to the town. While the deep mines have closed the town still retains the feel of a mining town. The pubs are mainly traditional and working men's clubs still flourish. Pigeon fancying and Staffordshire Bull-terriers go together in a Staffordshire mining community, and they are still the prized possessions of many an ex-miner.

Station Road in the 1950s.

Brick and tile production was a major industry in Hednesford. Many collieries had their own brickworks and the Cannock Chase Colliery Company was no exception. These extensive works were in production up to the '60s. After being used as a landfill, part of the site now houses the new stadium for Hednesford Town football club.

Cross Keys farmhouse is one of the oldest buildings in the town. The land surrounding the farmhouse has been used for housing.

The Cross Keys Inn dates back to 1746. The upper photograph is early '60s. The building at the rear of the car park was used by the football club and is now a restaurant. During the late '80s the future of the Cross Keys was in doubt, but public opinion and common sense prevailed and the building was restored for the enjoyment of future generations.

Splash Lane at the turn of the century, and as it appeared in early 1996.

The Accident Home was opened in 1886. Cannock Chase Coalowners Association was one of the organizations that supported the Home, as was the Blue Pilgrims, a religious order of nurses who did voluntary work at the Home. The site is now occupied by a small housing development.

This 1920s photograph is listed as 'man in road' and shows a typical street scene with the pub, chapel and houses with front doors opening on to the road. In fact this is Littleworth Road; the pub and chapel are still recognizable. The housing on the right has been replaced with an industrial estate.

Before the Great War Stafford Lane meandered through the fields with a stream. The stream remains, but with housing estates in place of fields, and the road is now a busy commuter shortcut to miss the town centre.

Cottages at Hill Top. The upper picture was probably taken in the early '60s; the DIY shop and the other stores closed in the late '80s. The cottages were being re-roofed when the lower shot was taken in early 1996.

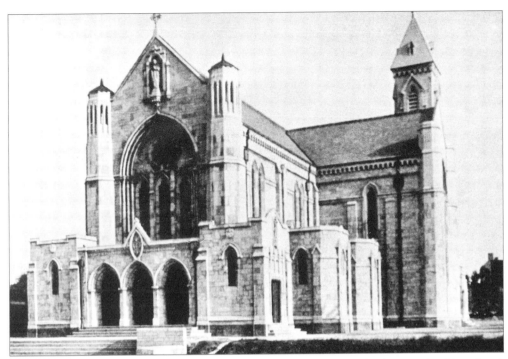

The major landmark in the town is this remarkable Roman Catholic church of Our Lady of Lourdes. A world-wide appeal for the funds was made by Father P.J. Boyle and construction started in 1926. The ambitious design was by G.B. Cox of Birmingham and is in the French Gothic style. In the hillside by the west door is the grotto of Our Lady of Lourdes. The upper picture is one of a set of four postcards sold for 6*d* when the church was consecrated by the Archbishop of Birmingham, Dr Williams, in 1934.

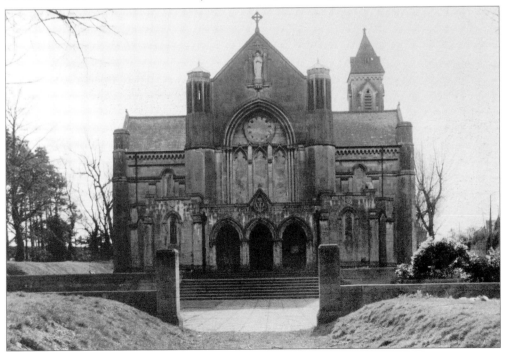

Hednesford war memorial stands at the top of an imposing pathway that leads from the gates on the Rugeley road. When this photo was taken in the late '20s there were fine views over the town from the memorial. Note the chimney of the Valley mine in the background.

The memorial in 1996. The tablet commemorating the fallen in the Second World War has been added.
The trees have grown and now block the views over the tower; a benefit is that they screen some of the
noise from the traffic on the A460.

Hednesford from Cockpit Hill. The house in the middle foreground has withstood change. The most noticeable new features are the shop/office block to the left of the house and the Post Office tower on the skyline.

The Valley Mine when it was being used as a training centre; it later became the mine rescue centre. When these activities were closed in the '80s the building was acquired by Cannock Chase Council and the Heritage Centre was started. This now includes the Museum of Cannock Chase, a Tourist Information Centre and the home of Heritage Independent Photographers.

The Ukrainian Club on the Rugeley road, 1907. The building was ex-RAF from Rugeley camp at Marquis Drive, known as Kit-bag Hill. One wonders if the similarity in shape of the new block of flats to this RAF hut is deliberate.

The level crossing where Marquis Drive crosses the A460 and the railway. The cottages in the upper photo are still there but cannot be seen from this viewpoint because of the high hedges.

Postcards were used to mark some quite gruesome events, including murder. This card detailing the murder of Mrs Gaskin by her husband in 1919 is a good example. The gas works where the body was found is now the site of an international company dealing in transmission systems.

Market Street, looking down the hill from near the present library. Apart from the new row of shops on the right most of the buildings remain. The noticeable changes are the shop signs. Luton House with its angled windows was Grosvenor and Cotterel, and is now Webb's Electrical Store.

At the bottom of Market Street, tucked away behind the shops, is Hednesford spiritualist church. The date of the upper photo is not known but there have been some recent modifications to the entrance in the lower shot (February 1996).

Market Street, looking towards the railway bridge. The buildings in this shot, while still recognisable as being the same, have been modernised. Modern Market Street was made into a one-way street from this point down to the crossroads on the A460 in 1991–2.

The Tudor-styled Anglesey Hotel was built in 1831 as a summer-house by Edmund Peel of Fazeley near Tamworth. It is now the headquarters of Pritchard Holdings, who operate many of the area's industrial developments.

Standing on the site now occupied by the Co-op 8 till 8 store, the Electric Palace was first a cinema and then a skating rink.

The station was a major factor in the town centre moving from the Cross Keys and Hill Top area to the north of the A460. The photograph on this page shows the station in the early 1870s when there was a level-crossing. The first bridge was built in 1875. The upper photograph on the opposite page dates from the 1930s, and shows a large group waiting for a train; this was probably a day trip for a local society. The present-day station is the terminus for the Hednesford to Walsall commuter route, which reflects the town's growing importance as a dormitory for Birmingham.

West Hill, now Green Heath Road, from the station bridge. The upper photograph dates from about 1890. Note the Beehive store on the corner (see pages 108 and 109). The lower photograph was taken in December 1995.

The old station bridge seen from Green Heath Road in the mid-'60s, and the new bridge which was finished in 1993 from the same viewpoint.

Beehive Corner at the junction of Cannock Road and Green Heath Road. The picture on this page shows the store before it was purchased by Clem Taylor and probably dates from before the Great War. The man in the apron standing in the doorway is Sid Harris, who continued working there after the shop was sold. The upper photograph on page 106 is one of the earliest showing the store. On the opposite page the two views show how this corner has changed. The upper photograph dates from just before the Second World War; the Beehive is clearly visible. The lower photo shows the empty plot where the store stood, and on the opposite side of the road John Hardman's has suffered the same fate.

The old police station in Cannock Road, now the offices of a furnaces brickwork construction company.

West Hill School in High Mount Street, shown before the Great War, is still recognisable today even with the new block that has been added.

The Royal George in High Town, which looks as if it doubled as a corner shop. This building is now a turf accountant's.

The Primitive Methodist chapel in Station Road. The small track up the side still exists alongside the new houses which have been built on the site of the chapel.

West Cannock mine, situated between Green Heath Road and Belt Road sometime in the '30s. Number 3 pit head is shown. The railway wagons were identified in large lettering to ensure their return to the correct colliery. The site is now largely grassed over and forms a pleasant local amenity, but the main buildings between Western Road and West Hill Avenue have been left as a derelict site.

RUGELEY

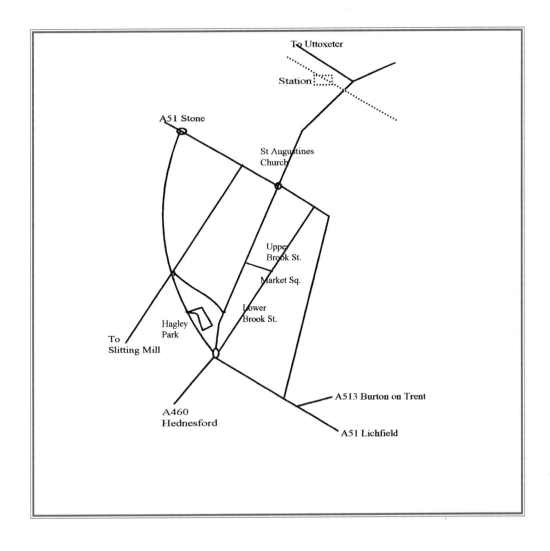

To Uttoxeter

Station

A51 Stone

St Augustines Church

Upper Brook St.

Market Sq.

Lower Brook St.

Hagley Park

To Slitting Mill

A460 Hednesford

A513 Burton on Trent

A51 Lichfield

Rugeley is a pleasant town which has retained some of its medieval layout despite two serious fires in 1649 and 1708. The centre of the town is a designated conservation area. Like Penkridge, Rugeley had a reputation for a good horse market in the seventeenth and eighteenth centuries. The town grew with the advent of the Trent and Mersey canal in the late eighteenth century, a process which continued when the Trent Valley railway line arrived in the nineteenth century.

The power station which dominates the skyline was, together with the now closed Lea Hall coal mine, the major source of employment from the end of the Second World War. The mine was sunk to supply coal to the neighbouring power station and closed during the early '90s along with part of the power station. New industry is being introduced on these sites.

Rugeley has also developed as a dormitory town for Birmingham, a feature of the towns bordering the Chase. Relatively easy road links with Birmingham, Derby and Stafford together with the pleasant countryside has made the Chase a popular area for commuters.

Rugeley marks the eastern side of the Chase, where the heather-and pine-covered hills meet the flat meadows either side of the river Trent.

Rugeley Trent Valley station.

Hagley pool appears on the first series Ordnance Survey map of 1834. The pool is now much smaller. The upper photograph only differs from the lower one in the size of the tree despite the forty-odd years between them. The park is now bisected by the bypass.

Brook House, Upper Brook Street, reputed to have been built for Viscount Anson in the 1880s. This Georgian building is now Grade 2 listed.

Lower Brook Street, looking towards Market Place. The left-hand side of the street has been replaced with the rather severe block of shops and offices, which contrast badly with the sensitive restoration on the opposite corner.

Market Place, *c.* 1920. The clock tower was built in 1879 as part of the indoor market, which has been replaced with a new market hall on the site of the Town Mill.

The background of the view from the railway in the '20s differs from today's. In the foreground the allotments have inevitably given way to housing. The tall spire belongs to the Roman Catholic church of SS Joseph and Ethelrade, built in 1849 by Hansom.

The charm of the '30s Trent Valley railway station has been replaced with this functional modern one on the electrified line to London from the north-west.

St Augustine's, the former parish church, was founded in about 1150. What remains dates mainly from the thirteenth century with the tower from the fourteenth century. The chancel window dates from about 1300. There is a gruesome memorial to Thomas Lauder (1670).

Just outside Rugeley on the A513 is Hawkesyard Priory and the adjoining house. Originally built by Lister in 1760 and known as Armitage Park, the house was bought by the widow of Josiah Spode III, the famous Stoke potter. Her son renamed the house after the medieval Hawkesyard which once stood on the site. The house was left to the Dominicans in his will in 1893 and they built the Priory. On completion of the Priory the house was yet again renamed, this time Spode House, and was used by the Order for conferences and retreats.

BRITAIN IN OLD PHOTOGRAPHS

To order any of these titles please telephone our distributor, Littlehampton Book Services on 01903 721596
For a catalogue of these and our other titles please ring Regina Schinner on 01453 731114